The Trembling Tiber

THE TREMBLING TIBER

A BLACK POET'S MUSINGS ON SHAKESPEARE'S JULIUS CAESAR

by

NEAL HALL M.D.

l'Aleph

NEAL HALL M.D.

THE TREMBLING TIBER

a black poet's musings on Shakespeare's Julius Caesar

Cover photo, courtesy of Julia Lehman Photography

2020 Published by l'Aleph – Sweden – www.l-aleph.com

l'Aleph is a Wisehouse Imprint.

ISBN 978-91-7637-588-4

CONTENTS

AUTHOR'S REMARKS

A N INCIDENT IN ROME, where I spent three months in 2016 as a visiting artist and scholar at the American Academy of Rome, triggered this exploration of Shakespeare's *Julius Caesar*. The Academy's director challenged the fellows to explore Rome, searching for inspiration that could inform our work. I took to wandering the city's streets.

One day, walking around the Academy's relatively affluent white neighborhood, I was stopped by a member of the Italian Special Forces. The soldier had his finger on the trigger of a semi-automatic rifle and demanded that I approach him. I refused, fearing any movement could be interpreted as provocation and thus justification for shooting me.

During my subsequent detainment, I kept asking myself what was the probable cause? I later realized it was my skin color. I had been profiled walking in the wrong place. The officer simply assumed I was an illegal African alien. My blackness seen walking in the wrong place was a sufficient visible marker for probable cause to detain me at near gunpoint.

By chance, that frightful color-coded indignity fell on the Ides of March, the day Caesar was assassinated, and this coincidence inspired "Probable Cause-III-XV, MMXVI," included in this collection. Writing "Probable Cause" whetted my appetite, prompting me to dig deeper into *Julius Caesar*. Shakespeare fascinated me. A student of human nature, he explored endlessly man's passions and what happens when they careen out of control. No element of the human condition or conflict was spared his attention: not love, death, injustice, revenge, grief, jealousy, murder, greed, treachery, reconciliation, nor forgiveness.

It was in his histories and tragedies, however, that Shakespeare crafted thinly veiled depictions of the current socio-political scene. In the parallels he drew between ancient Rome and Elizabethan England, he captured social and political conflicts that transcend time and lead to the shallow footprints we leave today.

Julius Caesar, especially, lends itself to comparison with our contemporary socio-political landscape. Studying the play with new eyes, it was clear that the parallels Shakespeare drew between the psychosocial-political makeup of ancient Rome and Elizabethan England persist today. For the alleged greater good, we continue to give lip service to moral standards while glossing over grievous infractions of basic decency and justice. We are still self-serving, self-aggrandizing. Political slogans like "Make American Great Again" echo Cassius's plea to return to a time when Rome was great and all power rested in the Senate, not in a would-be tyrant. Power is still used not to empower, but to overpower. Freedom is still circumscribed when self-determination is left to the luck of birth, when the deck is stacked and the race card trumps all. Romans looked down on non-Romans, called them barbarians and limited their rights.

Centuries later how different is gerrymandering that shuts people out of political and economic systems simply because, their ancestors were counted as only three-fifths human?

Julius Caesar drew me not simply by the richness of its content and insights into today's world. As a poet, I also wanted to immerse myself in the playwright's craft. *Julius Caesar* is rich in metaphors, puns, quotations, characters, and drama—the tools of Shakespeare's art. In this collection of poems, I have adapted passages from *Julius Caesar* to my purposes, adding imagery and casting the interpretations in my own metrical pattern of social commentary. In doing so, I have followed Shakespeare's lead.

Shakespeare's *Julius Caesar* was informed by Sir Thomas North's 1579 work, *Lives of the Noble Grecians and Romans*. The playwright is said to have copied and altered North's text at will, imposing his own wordsmithing and political observations.[1]

In this collection of poems, my words and wordplay intersect with Shakespeare's tools and wordplay. Interweaving Shakespearean tools with those of my own craft, I have composed hybrid poetic narratives that speak in direct and powerful new ways to universal contemporary issues of freedom and equality.

Vigilant of a balance between craft (wordplay) and content, I re-read *Julius Caesar* several times before selecting more than two hundred passages that fit within two categories:

1) Widely recognizable and celebrated passages like Mark Antony's funeral oration for Caesar: "Friends, Romans, countrymen lend me your ears"-Act 3, Scene 2, line 72;
2) Moving narratives like "The evil men do lives after them, the good is oft interred with their bones"-Act 3, Scene 2, line 74.

Five methods were employed to create hybrid poetic narratives:

3) Using the exact wording of a passage with its original intent. ("The Storm," for example, is composed using only words or phrases from the five passages in Julius Caesar that refer to a storm. No new words were added to create the poem and none eliminated.)
4) Changing the wording or sequence of a passage while retaining its original intent;
5) Changing the wording or sequence of a passage while creating an intent other than its original intent;

6) Using the same passage or derivative thereof in one or more poems ("Matriarchal Patriarch" and "He Said" both, for example, expand on the question of self-determination Shakespeare addressed throughout Julius *Caesar*. From "Matriarchal Patriarch," for example: "Fate is not in your stars/ but in part and parcel in you/that you are an underling";

7) Footnotes indicate where each excerpt or phrase originated.

The name Caesar is used throughout these poems. The specific context defines whether the Caesar is friend or foe, weak or strong, slave or slave master, liberty or tyranny. For example, in the poem "Naz," Caesar is a great man who passed due to an illness; in "The Trembling Tiber," Caesar is a slave struggling to be freed; whereas in "Let The Word Go Forth," Caesar is a tyrant.

Probing deep into Shakespeare's work, his craft and insights, challenged me to push the boundaries of my poetry and to experience different ways of seeing, knowing, and revealing. In the title of this collection I refer to the river that threads through Rome. This reference is more than geographic. The allusion to its turbulent waters is also a metaphor for social injustice, inequality, and marginalization. I tried to capture this metaphor visually in the cover photograph. When Cassius challenged Caesar to swim the Tiber in a violent storm, Caesar almost drowned. Similarly, the cover shows me struggling, naked in my vulnerability, our vulnerability, our struggle within the watery storm of subjugation.

My writings, informed by Martin Luther King, Malcolm X, and Gandhi, speak not just to the surface pain of injustice and inhumanity today, but probe deep into that pain we label and package into genteel socio-political-economic-religious constructs.

The parallels of *Julius Caesar* and this work reaffirmed my belief that the more things are said to change, the more things are made to stay the same by the powerful and the influential who enrich themselves by perfumed words, theft, betrayal, and deceit. The themes of *Julius Caesar* live amongst us still because our fears and greed dwell within us, still.

That Ides of March in 2016, I had experienced something in Rome that inspired me to turn to *Julius Caesar*. I then set out to explore how that play and other Shakespearean works could be contemporized to provide new prisms through which to view today's power constructs, how these tools might be adapted to illuminate the coded and decoded socio-political-economic struggles of marginalized people today. That journey deepened my recognition of the universality of man's nature and enriched my insights into the parallels of the universal struggles for freedom and equality across time, poignantly reminding me for whom liberty's bell truly tolls.

Neal Hall, January 2020
(www.nealhallpoet.com)

THE TREMBLING TIBER

sounds deafened, lungs depleted of air

a ceasar I, face down, sinking as deep
as my sunken heart sinks in me a
downward drift fathoms beneath
the torrent Tiber's raging maelstrom
of injustice, inequality, inhumanity

a ceasar I, a slave had not my life
been made to drown, face down,
the depths of blue watered under tides,
vexed and vortexed an ill-heart
and distempered contempt

stemming me, tempest-tossing me side to side[2]
this blue red sea black in me,

swallowed by its water
I've swallowed the waters
that have swallowed me, this
blue torrent turbulence black in me

sinking, no lifeguard I, a cassius,
who darest thou ceasar leap
and bade freedom a follow[3]

no life a lifeline I, a time
of martin, of malcolm, of gandhi,
souls committed this copious abyss
that does not render its dead[4] to
shoulder spent caesar, trembling[5]
a wretched slave's bent, broken body[6]
sinking, disposed of within the sinews
of the troubled Tiber[7], trembling,
tumultuous in its enormity

CURIA DI POMPEI[8]

democracy they queried
with lean and hungry looks,[9]
what conquest brings home you,
what tributaries follow you to rome
to grace in captive bonds your chariot wheels[10]

such men are dangerous who ask[11]
for they fear your crown fits
too well too many heads and too many
people rejoice too much in wanting
to wear your crown around their heads

despots have that lean and hungry look,[12]
conspiracy and ambition their thoughts
the meeting spot of theater'd justice,
the Curia di Pompei, that fateful place
where you, democracy, stood amidst
the intersect of:
passionate argument,
deviously placed forged letters,
a declaration of independence,
a soothsayer who tried to say
three times tyranny cries your crown
to pass around for fewer heads to wear
around their heads

there, you met the daggers' blades
the Curia di Pompei, that fateful place you,
democracy, stood amidst the intersect of

unread letters, warnings,
unheard cries of the people,
that fateful place, the intersect of
where they said all men when they
really did not mean all men

the intersect of
where they pretended to mend humanity's
tattered fabric with bendable words
from non-refillable pens of bendable men

the intersect of
manipulation and malicious persuasion,
traitors clothed in loose fitting confidants,
your crown to pass thrice around for
fewer heads to wear around their heads

fifty-one stabs, the Curia di Pompei,
'tis there, that crypt of betrayal amidst
the intersect of daggered deceit

AGAIN AND AGAIN

there is no amendment nor its
handgun instruments so fit a need its
amending as the second amendment[13]

if I thought prayer would move,
I'd be move to pray[14]when the
second amendment trumps the
sixth commandment to make
rich the thoughtless hands of the
most un-noble of bloodlines[15]

yet we offer our thoughts and prayers

when the gun has emptied its rounds
and its sounds transpose to those
slain about the ground, we then again
want to heal the gaping wounds within us
that persist daily amongst us

when the teleprompter prompts the reader
the abridged, made-for-TV, epitaphs,
we kiss dead caesars' wounds and dip scripted red
anger and anguish in betrayed desecrated blood[16]
to say on cue

our thoughts and prayers are with you
when they first thank first, the first
responders for responding first,
when they acknowledge first the
esprit de corps and cooperation of local
county, state and federal law enforcers who
enforced the full weight and force of their agencies
for violations of the sixth commandment whilst
overlooking the second amendment's
complicity in murder

our thoughts and prayers are with you
when they again want to know the motive,
the time frame, the response time within
the time frame to timely place rocks
on stars fallen untimely

again, our thoughts and prayers amidst
appalling silence, appalling apathy,
appalling complicity until an alleged shooter
whose purple hand reeks with gunsmoke[17]
shoots you, yours, to your appalling cries,
appalling disdain, appalling duplicity
as we bury your dead in our heads and
dare again offer our fleeting thoughts
and empty repeated prayers that fall
like the fallen falling on death ears
again and again to second amendment guns
and bullets amidst your thoughts and prayers

BEAR THESE TRUTHS

as you are the provocateur,
the agitator, the instigator,
tell me your truth

then as the provoker, agitator, instigator,
bear these truths I tell you[18]

I am not provocative,
I am the response to
your provocations

I am not militant
I am the response to
your militancy

I am not an activist,
I am the response to
being acted upon by you

BLACK HOLE

stared at blackness
from distant white stars,

I am a black hole alone, an
unknown intergalactic black,
a hued interplanetary view,
fearful falling through

gravitational slavery I am,
an event horizon[19] whose horizon
white and wanna-be white push
against being pulled into

invisible, internally reflecting no light,
no detectable features except black
stared at blackness too black that
black cannot by the glister of stars
give guess how near to day[20]

black hangs upon mine eyes[21]
too black for light and life
to be seen deep this black hole

CHEAP STREET DOPE

I will die to nothing
no heaven, no eternity
no serenity, no fear of hell

I know where to wear this dagger[22]

life bears too treacherous,
too bogus a hand[23]
I shall die wanting nothing

I'd rather my life not be lived in awe
of things that string pearls of nothing
falsely representing something that is not[24]

I know where to bear this dagger[25]

no peace, no joy
no crown my head
no lack of fearing

nothing to move me to smile at anything,[26]
not yearnings, not fantasies, not attired desires
not hope, not faith, not treachery of dreams[27]
not this cheap street dope men sell to and
make of other men

I will die to nothing,
life bears too brash,
too boisterous a hand[28]

bid its noise be still and all
be done in silence once again[29]

I shall die not as I have lived,
I know where to bear this dagger[30]

CLEAN FROM
THE PURPOSE

it's not that We love truth less
but that We love living a lie more:[31]

We The People, in order to appear
to have formed a more perfect union,
freely pretend and profess to establish
justice, ensure domestic tranquility,
provide for the common defense,
promote the general welfare,
secure the blessings of liberty[32]and
that all men abide these deeds but
We The People[33]

'tis marrow from feigned feeble tongues,[34]
there is but one mind in all these
We The People and it is bent[35]

men construing things after
their fashion clean from the
purpose of the thing itself,[36] 'tis
but a common proof of lowliness[37]

colorable, there is no black america,
no white america,
no latino america,

no asian america, there is but
the united states of America,[38]
more marrow from feigned feeble tongues[39]

We point a finger on the water's surface
and call it the moon
clean from the purpose
of the thing itself[40]

america was built on fear, not
on courage, imagination nor
an unbeatable determination[41] to not
point its finger on the water's surface
and call it the moon

clean from the purpose
of this thing itself[42]
let us start with truth,
to call it the lie:

We The People,
in order to form a more perfect union,
establish justice, ensure domestic tranquility,
provide for the common defense,
promote the general welfare, and
secure the blessings of liberty [43]
shrunken to this measure[44]
it's not that We love truth less
but that We love living the lie more[45]

Conspiracy O' Conspirators

friends, romans, countrymen,[46]
the ides of march have come
aye! tyranny but not gone,[47]

these men of senate, congress,
men of cloth, thou art ruins,
decayed chaffs of noblest men,[48]
composites fallen their pedestals
posing as marbled morale'd virtue

what republic can stand beneath
the misplaced awe of such men?[49]
honorable men who construe things
after their fashion, clean from
the purpose of the thing itself[50]

abusers their sacred station,
disjoining[51] right from righteous,
courage from courageous,
moral from morality,
equal from equality,
human from humanity,
robes and rosaries selling
off souls to a burning cross

greed be their ambition's ladder
whereto, in our foolish awe, they climb upward
turn their faces, but when they once
attain the uppermost rung, they
then unto the ladder turn their backs,
look in the clouds, scorning the base
by which they did ascend[52]

conspiracy, O' conspirators, thou
show only thy dangerous brow
by night when evils are most free
for conspiracy

and then by a day's light hide
in smiles, in affability,
in babies' kissed cheeks,
in rolled-up blue-collar sleeves,
to deceive an awed blue-collar
onlooker viewing a likeness of himself
in a rolled-up sleeved mirror of deception

these caverns deep, dark enough
to mask thy monstrous visage,[53]
cartels that do not tell,
they have not their look put upon their purpose,[54]
their armored theft of freedom

thou dangerous brow hidden by day's light
in perfumed wordplay embroideries, loosely
embroidered to easily unravel their promises

dangerous brows hidden in their
bipartisan pretense of aisled opposition
of themselves in stealth furtherance
to preserve division of our house
that it may stay fallen,

these caverns deep, dark
have not their look put upon
their hidden purpose[55]

these men of senate, congress,
men of cloth, abusers of disjoining powers[56]

the ides of march have come
aye! tyranny but not gone,[57]

friends, romans, countrymen,[58]
conspiracy O' conspirators
slaves in bondage deliver
slaves from bondage[59]

every bondman in his
own hands bears the power
to cancel his captivity[60] of
conspiracy O' conspirators

CROWN OF EQUITAS[61]

three times
theocracy, tyranny and tyrants tempted,
you be the sole bearer this crown[62]

thrice tried this trio thy hand be tied,
and three times by the back of thine hand
you did not put by the offer[63] sworn
to be worn the heads of all

thus I this plea to Equitas,
his noble girth my right of birth
of equal time and worth to
wear upon my head that which
you wear unwell upon yours

I, no hour as fit as this hour,[64] do open my mouth
to beg the voice and utterance of tongue[65] to grit
into my teeth[66] a mournful plea, O' yea wreath
I, too, to wear your one-jeweled crown
sworn to be worn the heads of all

I a plea this feathery weight of equal weight that is
but a feather's weight when worn in parity,
when borne we together upon leveled shouldered men
bearing equal heads to rest the laureled headdress Equitas,

lined in gilded-leafed equality, dignity, humility
upon all heads, you wear unwell upon yours

three times I, a plea to Equitas his noble girth,
my right of birth claimed now,
worn now to one head, your head,
sworn to be worn the heads of all, which
you wear unwell upon yours

CRYING FIRE

you can with bad haste and ignitable straw
keep a raging four-hundred-year fire[67]
of division, racism, anti-semitism ablaze

but you can't cry fire in a crowded theater

you can lie and cry a caravan of
brown invaders, funded by hebrews,
is invading the southern white borders of
the true and original hordes of white invaders

but you can't cry fire in a crowded theater

you can lie and cry a racist hoax that
brown folks bespoke in red coats
are coming to kill white folks

you can lie and cry terrorists, jihadists,
are hiding in the midst of a lawless caravan but

you can't cry fire in a crowded theater

you can throw black and hebrew red meat to
awaken, stoke, incite, radicalized hibernating
ravenous racist radicals

but you can't cry fire in a crowded theater

first amendment protection of free speech
does not protect dangerous speech directed
at inciting mayhem, death,
falsely shouting inflammatory
cries of fire in a crowded theatre[68]

you can't be a liar crying fire,
divisive lips can't from their divisiveness cry fire[69]
in a crowded theater of divided states,
united against one another

it's actionable, punishable;
an imminent lawless action limiting
the lair's racist first amendment rights[70]
to cry aloud fire in a crowded white theater

DARKENED FOOLS[71]

all our yesterdays which darken us fools
creeps this[72] place poverty, made more impoverish,
made more amiss day to day to make
our tomorrows made more foolish
to make more of us lasting fools

this forged freedom, a fading
shadow's blackened silhouette
which art our dearth, our predestined death

poor prayers[73] praying unanswered prayers, we
strut and fret fleeting seconds upon freedom's stage[74]

players played by players
full of sound and fury signifying nothing,
then we are heard no more,[75] downwardly
down this continuous trail of darkened fools

Democracy II

democracy,

simulated, incandescent, luminescent,
brought forth the adder to
singularly shine its predacious
day upon the weary walker[76]

democracy,

a mendacious mandate of "all"
that does not include all men,
excluding black men

a manifesto of an oath, of hope, equality
with no declared delivery date, time, for those
haggardly steps of the oligarchy's negro,
brand-named the mark and seal of the
bill of sale and purchase bequeathed "all"
the sons of democracy's founding fathers:

washington, jefferson,
franklin, jackson

democracy,

an oligarch's sleight of hands note of hand[77] treaty,
tampered with, trampled on by the tips of
thick-tongued, double-speaking triple talk
tongue-tied within their centrifuged untruths

democracy,

a manifesto of broken dreams, false hope,
jim crow status quo declared and delivered
those shallow steps of the black negro

brutus hath a suit that caesar will not grant[78]

DENY DENY

I don't remember, I don't recall

I have not a width of hair of that
to remember[79]

I have no memory of that and
my memory has no memory of
not recalling not remembering

I have no memory and
there is no evidence to
suggest that I do

DOG-WHISTLING

monkey this up dog-whistling,
a KKK thought bubble bursting,
exploding across KKK lips,
decoded, loaded, racially charged kindling,
to ignite the base to get the base out to vote,
not on morality, not on intellect,
not on temperament but on color,

not on equality, not on justice,
not on liberty, but on color

inciting havoc,
unleashing the dogs of war[80]dog-whistling,
that high-pitched low sound,
howling the blue-collared hounds to black it up
whistling monkey this up

dog-whistling the dogs and
when called out, disingenuously
walk back the diss,[81] apologize,
say it was a mistake,
say it was a figure of speech,
say it was an unconscious slip of
racially charged consciousness
tossing charred red meat to feed
racially ravenous dogs

when called out walk it back,
slither back and say let's move
on for the good of the country
monkeying it up, dog-whistling

DUE TAGLI

steadfast bucephalus,[82]
my steed, my pegasus,[83] though
thou be ancestral greek,
roman words will I, in part, speak

hear me, receive me for this
cause that calls in me,
be thee swift afoot to that
you bear[84] on you that lies in me,

be steadfast this vanguard steed,
your stalwart back I bestride, clasping
gladius's[85] hilt[86] firm about its grip[87]
that sits majestically on guard
affixed its medaled cross guard[88]

stride me swiftly this saddle seat and
question not in canter nor bite of bridled bit
the necessity of our gallop and gallantry[89]

steadfast bucephalus,[90] we are as
hephastion[91] and alexander were to
achilles and patroclus,[92] united as one,
striding as one, fighting as one

we are the single mind of the
double-edged blade libertas,
its strong side the strong
taglio[93] of due tagli[94]

steadfast bucephalus, my steed, my pegasus,
with hands, hearts, and hooves,
let us be liberators thrust deep within rhythmically
pulsed blood-filled atriums and ventricles

let us be liberty's gladius, sheathed its tip [95]
to bear no rud drip, our brothers' blood

steadfast my steed, steadfast

DUPED OR WILLFULLY WITTING

sheep or wolves in sheep's clothing,
politicians would not be wolves but for the fact
that they know the public to be sheep[96]
or wolves in sheep's clothing

we the public, pretenders this mask
we wear as our true face, pegged
petty men seen peeping about,
beneath, between the huge legs of fate,[97]
eyes wide open, pretending to be blind,
seemingly resigned to accept the lies,
the betrayal of public office by
public servants, stating, pledging
oaths to those sacred duties
public office holds

duped or willfully witting, we all
see welfare or the illusion of it
in those white-collared lies adorned
in alternating days of red or blue ties

oppressed or guileful opportunist
we all see welfare or the will-o'-the-wisp
in flagged-pinned labels and a
penned pipe dream of we the people

nostalgic, nationalist, narcissistic refrains of
we want to make america strong again,
we want to put america back to work again

we want to go back again to when
america was greatest, when
the least of them were colored men

politicians would not be wolves
but for the fact that they know we
are sheep or wolves in sheep's clothing,[98]

they know we are the seeds of greed
they can sell a field of dreams to,
to cause us to easily accept the lies,
the betrayal of public office by
public servants stating, pledging
us an oath to those sacred duties
public office holds that we dupe ourselves,

that we willfully wittingly lie to ourselves
are truths held not in ourselves but in
our dreaded stars hung above our heads

FAILING TO SEE

vision fair and fortune,[99] our eyes
failing to see in things reflecting its eyes,
reflecting in the eyes of others[100]

night hangs low below our eyes,[101]
we have not in them paired
oneness and show of unity
they were born of[102] and whose
optics doth lose its bend of awe
and singular focal point[103]

severed from ourselves with a
downward look on ourselves
we fail to see we are the
predator and prey[104] of ourselves

we are at war with ourselves
failing to see we are at war
against ourselves[105]

insight no more within our sight,
our eyes, sightless to our brothers'
timeless trail of tears, have not
our sympathetic grieve nor weep[106]

in greed have we wasted eternities of
freedom[107] purchasing favorable opinions
from gray-haired voices, looking empty
past men's seven deadly sins[108] to
payments passed beneath the table, to
deceivingly say our worse deeds[109] are good

many a man comes rapacious to bathe his
insatiable hands this sanguineous fountain
of greed spurting greened blood he
can never drain his stained hands of[110]

had we as many honorable eyes as these
horrid hands, we would see ourselves
reflecting in one another's eyes[111]

vision fair and fortune,[112] our eyes
fail to see in things reflecting its eyes,
reflecting in the eyes of those
we pray to pluck, then prey upon[113]

GODS AND LEADERS

white man tells us
what our gods and leaders
look like

therein they, weak men,
make themselves appear
most strong

therein they, tyrants,
make themselves appear
magnanimous gods[114]

mirage'd,[115] they then stand
like true gods and leaders

deluded[116] by delusion,[117] we
prostrate before them, thinking
them to be our gods, our leaders

HE SAID

he said

all we say to america is to be
true to what you said on paper[118]

because, he said, somewhere I read you said
all men, not just white men, you've
created equal with inalienable rights[119]

somewhere, he said, I read you said
three-fifths did not exist anymore
with your abolishment of slavery[120]

somewhere I read you said
we had the measured right against
unreasonable searches and seizures[121]

somewhere I read you said
we had a right to fair trial
by a jury of our peers[122] and that
we are innocent until proven guilty,
not by an absence of whiteness

somewhere I read you said
there would be no gerrymandering nor
color-coded poll taxes to undermine
one man, one vote of every black man[123]
somewhere I read you said
on parchment, on papyrus,
on your letterhead paper that we
hold these truths to be self-evident
and now is their necessity[124]

and all we've said to democracy was somehow,
somewhere, be true to what you said on paper[125]
because he said:
there would be difficult days
that lie lay ahead but it really didn't matter to him,
he'd been to the mountaintop
he said he did not mind, like anybody,
he wanted to live a long life,
longevity had its place but he
was not concerned about that

said he just wanted to do his god's will
and that his god allowed him
to go to the mountaintop

and that he looked over and he had
seen the promised land; he said
that he might not get there with you

but wanted you, the black man, white man
jew, gentile, muslim and hindu to know
that we as a people would get to the promised land

said he was happy, he was
not worried about anything

he was not fearing any man, his eyes had seen
the glory of the coming of his lord[126]

and an angered scowl did plow democracy's
brow a lean and hungered look[127] and
starred it upon the King with ungentle eyes,[128]

and with one shot, they shot him,
dropped him there on that spot
where he said we've got some
difficult days that lie ahead

and today, all we say to democracy
is somehow, somewhere, be true
to what you said on paper[129]
he said

His Bellow, Nigger

within well-established emerald grass[130]
institutionally rooted in tilled black top soil[131]
hidden below heavily packed white snow,[132]
the snowman[133] covers his bellow, nigger,
in pristine saintly surface white whisperings
of n-word and negro

infrequent the occasions and not oft
have we climbed martin's mountain [134]
to sound the shofar[135] so thunderously that
freedom, hearing the reverberance of our dissonance,
quakes[136] and cracks blacken soil an avalanche[137] for
heavily packed white snow to slither and slide the land
exposing tilled, raked top-soiled niggers
snowmen root their emerald grass to
bear greed as flint bears a fire[138]

all doings done beneath pristine surface white
pretending it did not know that
top-soiled niggers existed anymore
in the continuous cold winter of america
and the infrequent occasions of our
sounding the shofar

HOMELESS

homeless, my loins have no home

fatherless, no father, so I don't know
what it's like to be a son
and no sons, so I don't know
what it's like to be a father

no house to hold, no household,
no haven to call heaven

homeless, no motherland to
breastfed me, to tell me
who my fathers were,
whom I' m son to, from what seeds
my sons could have come

homeless, landless, neither home nor land
to leave a son so I did not have one

'tis theft these thieves that
I know not the roots of my seed nor
that black soil they were ripped from[139]

fatherless, no father,
so I don't know what it's
like to be nor have a son,

I don't know what it's like
to be a father

fatherless, sonless,
homeless, landless,
neither home nor land
to call my motherland

KAEPERNICK[140]

lest we forget,
that lofted flag affords us
the right and protection
to kneel one knee before it
in protest of all its anthem'd,
stand-hand-over-heart wrongs
perpetuated to symbolic melodic refrains
of symbols of, but not the living up to
what the hand-over-heart symbol stands for

shall rome stand under one anthem's awe[141]

symbolic standing to symbols,
not achieving them, not living them
is complicity in inhumanity[142]

for beneath thy best anthem'd apparel
and appearance, thou art still thou[143]

tyranny, slaver

LET THE WORD GO FORTH

leeched of history and heritage,
we've been terrorized twenty score years
of tortuous tasks and the brutal lash
by callous task masters

black men, countrymen,
I and you and all of us, plebeians of rome,[144]
noosed our gullets to captive bond,
cogs in caesar's chariot wheels whilst
tyranny, disguised, draped in a robe of
a republic rules our day[145] a tyrant

and we had rather be dogs
whimpering at half the light of a full moon
than a pack of wolves bearing our canines,
growling, howling a howl so loud at our darkness[146]
that the tiber would tremble at its banks
and make concave its shores, resonating
the replications of our growls[147]

black men, countrymen,[148]
I and you and all of us, our lives made
dispensable, valueless to be made cash
redeemable by tyrants belying democracy

thus from us, let the word go forth
that this part of tyranny we do bear,
we can at our pleasure shake off[149] to be
the scrum of unrelenting wolves, packed
in prowl and pursuit their prey, freedom

let the word go forth that no stony tower,
no walls of beaten brass, no airless dungeon
no strong links of iron can restrain nor constrain
our strength of urgency to be free

let the word go forth, let every nation know,
we will no longer permit the continued
undoing of our right to be, which this caesar
has long committed itself in denying
and living in denial with itself[150]

let the word go forth, we will no longer be
abel to cain to enable cain, nor remus to
romulus only to have rome draped in republic

let every person, every nation know
whether they wish us well or ill that we shall
defy paying any price, avert any hardship,
lay siege against any burden, support any
friend, oppose any foe to assure our
liberties and justice for all men[151]

let us not be dogs whimpering at the moon but
this warrior wolf pack,[152] canine'd and howled

let us be gladius[153] in the hands of gladiators,
growling at the moon, mutually pledging
our lives, our fortunes, our sacred honor[154]

let these words go forth from the air
in our lungs to friend and foe alike, that
the torch of urgency has been lit,
it burns fiercely now eternally[155] to let every
caesar know that this part of tyranny that
we do bear, we can at our collective pleasure
shake off,[156] be these ronin[157] wolves, canine'd,
packed in pursuit of our prey, freedom

MANGER OF HATE

littered the lawns of the appalling silent,
heard I, many of the best of rome
speaking of freedom and democracy
whilst groaning beneath their silence,
the want of no more talk of it[158]

you say hate has no home here[159] but
that does not make your hate homeless
and without a homeland here

for out of you comes forth to me
your savior hate that you choose to use
to rule and rape the land of gold;
your precious savior, your king of kings,
your luminary hung luminous in the
lower hemisphere you look up to sink into

hate, not an affliction of your mind but
your mind's affection you give birth to,
here in a stolen manger, in a stolen stable built
on stolen land by slave labor of stolen people
overseen by magi overlords pendulously swaying
frankincense ascending to ashen heaven, your
hued inheritance, your entitled pension,
your believed right of dominance[160]

you, the best of rome,[161] unwise men smearing
manure'd myrrh to put a more pleasant scent
to the pungent suffering and decay of our bodies
in bondage from your hate born here

you say, hate has no home here,[162]
but your saying it does not make
your hate homeless and without
a homeland here, littered on the
lawns of your appalling silent

MATRIARCHAL PATRIARCH

fate is not in your stars
but in part and parcel in you,
that you are an underling[163]

the hand he raises is made of
the same hand you raised

you gave birth to,
breastfed, and raised
his hand

fault is not in fate[164]
but, in part, in you

you, this grievous weight-bearing arch
shouldering a patriarchal fist,

it's you who teaches the son
it's his hand that sees in plain view
your hand when you raise your hand
against his sister, your sisters,
your daughters-in-law

you can't demand your yoke be lifted
while you yoke your sisters beneath you

fault is not in fate
it grows in you, you gave birth to,
breastfed, and raised the man
who raises his hand

fate and fault are not constellations
but a distillation, a condensation of
culturalized, traditionalized condemnations;
birthed, breastfed to raise the backside
of its hand to your daughter's face that she
comes to know his will and her lowly place

it's you, your hard-handed handiwork
mandating domestic vocations over
economic emancipation from his high-handedness

it's you, the pretty ones
and ones the pretty ones say
are not so pretty

it grows in you in hues of light,
lighter and the lightest of white,
it's your black specter cast from your black sun
beneath which the contours of your
dalit sister's darker darkness can't shadow
your deep well waters of matriarchal
privileges of light and lighter without being
brutalized within inches of her life

it's you, your lipstick'd matriarchal arithmetic
dividing, subtracting meager domestic wages on
a niggardly patriarchal abacus that does not add up
nor divide out evenhandedly from your hand

it's you, your hand that demands your
handmaid sisters enter separate doors to sit
lowly your floors before separate plates,
separate knives, separate forks, separate glasses,
made to eat separately sitting
your cold matriarchal floors,
too many their bodies your floors, sitting there

too many of their hopes your floors,
dying there, and you wonder why
he raises his hand at you,
you, the mother of daughters and daughters-in-law,
you who desecrate every universal law of dignity
against your daughters, your daughters-in-law

fate is not in fault
and fault is not in fate[165]
they're seeds in you that grow in you,
your daughters, your daughters-in-law
who grow to become mothers and
mothers-in-law who violate every
universal law of humanity against
their daughters, their daughters-in-law

you can't demand the man above you
to lift his yoke from you while you
yoke the woman beneath you

it's his eyes of his hand
that watch your hand clench
a matriarchal fist of misogyny

it's you who teaches the son,
you who gave birth to,
breastfed, and raised his hand
that demands the dowry,
burns your flesh, splashes acid to you
and your daughter's face

it's your hands, it's in your hands that
first uncle's hands first rape your first daughter
for the first time and her tears cry to try
to tell you for the first time and your first reply
to her tear filled eyes is to bear this and
bury it in the wounds of her womb and
never speak of it a second time

fault is not in fate
fate is not in fault, but in part, in you,
growing in you that
you are his underling[166]

it grows in you, you gave birth to,
breastfed, and raised the man
who raises his hand against you

fate is not in your stars
but, in part and parcel, in you,
that you are an underling[167] of
your raised hand against you

MULLIGANS

born again profiteering false prophets
professing to protect the unborn only
to undo them, undermine them,
mine them monetarily once
the unborn is born time again

holier-than-thou hooligans who,
when all life is pro-life, when
both are two lions born of the same litter,[168]
fight for the welfare of the fetus
but not welfare for the newborn

holier-than-thou hooligans
passing out evangelical mulligans
to impious charlatans peddling
sanctimonious pro-life demagoguery

holier-than-thou hypocrites, pimping
spurious sentiments and sacraments
to protect the unborn only to undo them,
un-voice them, undermine them, divide them
by race, class, and choice in order to monetarily
abort the unborn once the cord cuts them newborns,
this, the unkindest cut of all[169]

NA RAZ[170]
4.23.17

neither heaven nor earth has
been at peace this night,[171]
the fall leaf letting go its hold
to fall the branch it hung its life from

itself a holy grail, he nailed himself
upon a cross, a savior for his family

Caesar 'tis stricken[172]

three parts him heaven already
and the man entire, upon his last cry
na raz yields him home[173] as the
heavens called his name in songs
in a tongue more melodic than all
the melodies ever heard a Caesar[174]

mercifully, the gods so sped him
as he cried relief granted forgiving peace
more than the fear his death[175]

Caesar 'tis stricken[176]

his judgment that ruled our hands,
our youth, and wildness shall
no whit appear and will but all
be buried his gravity, his grave[177]

Jacob climbed his lowered ladder and
from his broad wings plucked his flightless
feathers to fly him a higher pitch home[178]

peace, home, Caesar 'tis stricken[179]
and speaks[180] na raz, na raz

and our father, now who art in heaven
and we are governed by our mother's spirit[181]

his bones to rest that hath
but labored lifelong to attain
his hour's last creed [182] na raz[183] to
go back to where he came from

ORIGINS IN ME

up babel's tower, through troy
and jericho and windowed
western wailing walls with the
need to know in my arms

there have I sat the lifelong day,
waiting with impatient wanting
to see with orphaned eyes, to know[184]
the origins in me

44 percent nigerian in me
28.9 percent sierra leonean in me
14.9 percent kenyan in me
1.3 percent central american in me

10.9 percent british, irish in me,
transatlantic high sea Mengeles,
overseers of slaves and rape by
such men as these whose swords
were whetted, made rich with the blood
of my fathers, my mothers[185]

such men as me can never be at
mind's ease,[186] having climbed those
walls, those towers, to discover the
origins in me of such men as these

OVAL-OFFICE ORAL LIES

ambitious mischief take what
liberties of truth thou wilt[187]

thou profess nobility yet I
see thy honorable metal be
wrought from that noble shape
you claim disposed of[188]

an investment in myth
an alternative reality, a realignment of lies,
to appear to be reality with his hand
ever so slightly touching the bible

oval-office oral lies,
an inventor of tales and libeled myths with
his misspoken hand only slightly on his bible

a genius of being disingenuous
bending facts, detached from facts,
detracting, distracting, deconstructing a fact
to be an artifact of a fact not factually exact

a narrowed parsing of the truth
misremembering, a momentary lapse
of amnesia sticking sticky falsities

upon the people's chair
in the people's house to stick to
the people's statue of liberty [189]

thou profess nobility yet I
see thy honorable metal be
wrought from that noble shape
you claim disposed of[190]

if we won't call them lies
why should he

treachery tittering from the
tip of the tongue, tossing oval-office,
oral lies into open windows
of narrowed minds

veracity vestured by distorted reality,
a denial of reality, a recasting of reality,
a short-sighted short bet indebting truth
to lies truth can't write a check against

veracity shrouded selling untruths
known to be not true to an unwitting,
witless base in hope of gaining,
at a lesser truth, a more profitable advantage,
fraudulently appearing to be a higher truth
but never a lie, never a liar

PRETEND

virtue knows it to be
your outward façade whilst
inside your hide,

you hide good keep,
your trail of betrayal,[191]
setting honor to your false eye,
glass and treachery to your other
all-seeing one[192]

good men, know you pretend, pretending
not to see the wrongs done since you've no
silver-mirrored reflection to reflect
your unworthiness into your best eye
that sees not of itself[193]

so as by my reflection, I your
true glass to see through to
view that of yourself that
you deny in good pretense
of yourself[194]

PROBABLE CAUSE—III-XV, MMXVI

I, the face of Othello,
a night without moon nor star
the absence of white the knife
thou does thrust—et tu, brute
its deep depth

I, the race of Othello,
a melanin tone that drones the mono-toned
standard permitting under-toned armed prerogative
unreasoned warrant my suspect

ill-lighted I am the preponderance,
that standard of criminality they
want to stand when night is made to
stand before a day's hued judgment

Othello's face, I am this preponderance of evidence
day walkers need no warrant issued, except
the warrant to want to not see the dead of night
rise a daylight participant in a worldwide daydream
of america-like greed

when the eyes of march are judges and jurists
black is the preponderance of evidence
whites need see for probable cause;
cause to violate black, black persons,
black houses, black papers, black effects,
with unreasonable searches and seizures; the
knife thou does thrust its deep depth
the dead of night

no oath nor affirmation need be
other than their pledge of
their lives, their fortunes, their sacred honor,
to this discrete dishonor, particularly describing
black places, black faces, black things
for search and seizure

I, the face of Othello, a fellow of the night,
the preponderance of flawed evidence
whites see as probable cause when the
eyes of march be judges and jurists

PROTEST MARCH

tired, valiant foot soldier,[195] whose
foot march has no forward footmarks

a gray emaciated whiskered stallion, sunken,
saddled from withers' end to coupling[196]
a low sitting, slow-riding saddle of resistance
we've ridden far too long, far too far
down this road, up this hill

it does not respond to the reins pulled,
turned the way of the bit it bites
nor our spurs to urge it on
down this road, up this hill

its gallop a cantor, its cantor a walk,
its walk a three-legged stance that
does not take any other stance which
hath its hour with every man[197]
down this road, up this hill

this march, this protest march,
a tired, valiant foot soldier[198] I've to
put to pasture that it comes to know
the end its day's business; that its day
has ended and the end is known[199]

RACE CARDS

privileged in this, who are you
that calls me,[200] accuses me
of playing the race card
pulled from a deck of 51
white playing cards bearing
your palm's print alone[201]

your faces held close your chest,
one by one,[202] one after the other
pulled without the shuffle,
from the bottom of your deck to do
your hands' color-coded business

more white than red and blue,
your back side declared in red, white and blue

how many ages shall we hence,
this one card, be acted[203] upon
by 51 dealt you to pull,

you, that calls me,[204] accuses me
of playing the race card
pulled from a deck of 51
white playing cards bearing alone,
your palm's print

REVERED RIDE

he did not cry liberty, freedom,
tyranny[205] is afoot for me

revered paul revere's ride
was not a ride for me,
not a cry for me

his stead, brown beauty[206]
was not in full stride for me

he, of these men that
gave their country liberty,[207]
he did not ride for me,
did not cry out to me
when the british, when the dutch, when the portuguese
came for me with slavery, looking for slaves

he did not cry from sea to shining sea
murder, rape, slavery, thou art afoot
from sea to shining sea for me

he did not cry now is the necessity[208] for me
by any means necessary[209] for me
he did not cry—look out! riding, striding
up Look Out Mountain[210] for me

paul revere's ride was not
a revered ride for me,
he was not my savior crying out
to save me from the british, the dutch, the portuguese
who came for me

he did not cry out to me
he did not ride brown beauty full stride for me
when white tyranny came ashore looking
for black slaves, for black slavery for me

RODS AND CONES

rods, cones—photoreceptors—
paired transmitters of dim wit light
into electrochemical sight and insight of a
clearer visualization, a deeper appreciation
of all hues of humanity seen the visual cortex,
that sooth seer who bids beware Cain's eyes of march
laid upon me to march me into mental slavery[211]

white, that Cain against his brother Abel,
that came, robbed my cones to leave me rods,
dark their outer sight to make me see only
white's black in that special-made black
made for me, brewed for me, brewed in me,

that processed black tea, that black decaffeinated
coffee poured pasteurized white cream to ensure
my deep passive, pacifist blind-eyed sleep seeing
not itself but what other eyes tell it to see of itself[212]

white came in Cain, took my cones,
made a colored man to see only in
well-defined lines of black and white,
well-defined dividing lines dividing black into white,
dividing, misaligning universal black into a negro
wanting to be, needing to see phenotypic white

Cain came with well-demarcated lines,
absent shades of grey to make clearer
who is the white master,
who, the black slave,
who is wretched, who well-made,
who is second-class citizen,
whose self-image is imbued
in that brewed view of black
made third person by first-class, first-person
white persons who came to rain
Cain against their brother Abel

RULES OF LAW

rules of law, enthroned rigged veracity,
thy ambitions take what liberties of
verities thou wilt,[213] I know virtue not to be
in your caesars and their senates,
prevaricators, promiscuous with facts but
never misleading, never misrepresenting,
never liars, never lies disguised
in more lies lying, they are not lies

entitled to your own opinions whilst
titled heirs to fabricated facts spewed as truths
to break laws within the rule of law, looped
holes to circumvent the rule of law

I know virtue not to be[214] in your
caesars and their senates,[215] whose
mouths yawn and yield up[216]
personal ambitions, tongue-tied to lies
in your rules of laws rulers misuse
to rule over the powerless to enrich
themselves of commonwealth

rulers of rules of law set truth
to their one eye false,
fallacy to the other all seeing eye,[217]

their short-sighted short bets indebt[218] them
to lies they cannot cash cheques against,
selling charades they know to be lies

theirs are lies but never misleading,
promiscuous with the facts but
never lies, never liars, never prevaricators
disguised in more lies lying, the
rules of law are not lies, in order to say
no laws were disobeyed

Si Vis Bellum Para Pacem[219]

no feather crosses unsevered
the unsheathed blade of a sword

warriors of peace know
history is replete with hate
triumphing over love

warriors of peace know war
to be the answer, love is not,
for love has never fully conquered hate
what conquest has love brought to peace?

what enslaver graced in captive bonds
to love's chariot wheels trails laureled love
bearing peace to lay at our fettered feet?[220]

it is not that I love love less
but I know hate to be greater,[221]
history is replete with hate
prevailing over love
Jesus, Martin, Malcolm, Gandhi -
no feather crosses unsevered
the unsheathed blade of a sword

we've been deceived, lead to believe
love conquers hate when it's gluttony
that massa mastered to master our fate
that we mistake as massa's hate

warriors of peace know that
it's not a love-hate war, that
freedom like peace comes at a price,
a price to obtain it, a price to sustain it

a warrior knows the war is an economic war
it was massa's economics that enslaved us
it will be our economics that will free us from massa

this is not a love-hate war
it's an economic war waged pharisees
who've sown their seeds four-folds
in their brothers' misery

its slaveholders refusing to let go their
hold of gold coast slaves made to crawl
moiling gold in colonial strongholds
of new world windfalls

a warrior knows if you want peace, war
awakens, speaks, strikes, redresses[222]

war cries, one by one, give me your hands,[223]
here we point our swords,[224] this
the most liberating cut of all,[225]
for arms, hands can do no more harm
when the head is cut its shoulders[226]

a warrior rather tell thee what it is to be feared
than what it is to fear[227]

warriors of peace know it's an economic war
doused in accelerants—divisiveness, intolerance—
that insatiable, heartless capitalists set
ablaze to distract us from and to destroy
the proof of truth that the answer
is in our economics, not in our love

love cannot conquer greed nor hate
what conquest has love brought to freedom?
what enslaver graced in captive bonds
to love's chariot wheels trails laureled love
bearing freedom to lay at our fettered feet?[228]

warriors of peace know there is no
peace without some measure of war

warriors know it's not a hate-love war
it's an economic war

a warrior knows an economic force
equal to or greater than the economic force
that strikes against you is greater
than love's capacity to free you

no feather crosses unsevered
the unsheathed blade of a sword

if you want peace
prepare for war[229]

a warrior knows,
a warrior of peace knows

SLAVE TRADE

four downs to touchdown
twenty-four seconds to hit massa's three,
three strikes to run four white bases home

homegrown, homeless gemstone gladiators,
inner city preyed-on playground substrate,
netted, playing in prefabbed unnatural habitats ported
new world order slave ships:
NBA, NFL, NL, AL,
like old world order slave ships:
JOL,[230] MDD,[231] HM,[232] DDM[233]

all hands on deck turning
cold sordid waters
into cheap white wines

all hands on deck mining african blood diamonds
to ship to cultivate in coliseum'd high schools,
collegiate plantations, weighted in auction-block audits
and good measure wait to be stripped, pinched, padded,
prodded, trotted for limp, licked for salt content

all their hands on deck selecting,
weeding, breeding-out intrinsic intellect, that
precursor of independent thinking, reasoning the
overseer fears will unravel his hand-woven neo-slavery,
fears the unraveling of drafting neo-negroes on
neo-auction blocks where neo-slaves are bought
and sold, branded, enumerated, uniformed

how many ages hence shall we, this
dreadful scene be acted upon our
newborns yet to be born playing on
playground plantations yet to be born?[234]

odds-on favorite the odds are stacked against their favor,

a one-in-a-million chance to be salary capped blacks,
massa-made "all-starred," "all pro" mandingo[235] heroes
to displace and replace displaced black mothers,
black fathers with MVP inner city negro cargo
owned by neo-slave masters neo-slave trading
neo-negro cargo preyed on, netted the neo-slave ships
NBA, NFL, NL, AL, iconic acronyms for the true
ballers playing niggers between the whistle,
enshrining them a hall of fame house to house
house niggers the overlord let off his cotton fields
to build his house a bigger house to build
a larger storehouse to house and store
his neo-negro cargo to shuffle

four downs for a touchdown
twenty-four seconds to hit massa's three,
three strikes to run four white bases home

NBA, NFL, NL, AL, the real ballers,
Casca, Cinna, Cassius
Ligarious, Metallus, Trebonius
and et tu, Brute,[236]
all the same daggers when it pleases[237]
them to befall black caesars[238]

how many ages hence shall we, this
dreadful scene be acted upon our newborns
yet to be born, licked for salt content, playing
on playground plantations yet?

SPEAK

romans, countrymen, black men,
lend me your ears that I might better
hear that you hear me well[239]
caesar doth bear us hard[240]

who is he that loves liberty
more than he fears slavery?[241]

who is he a starved mouth that
spews the husk to eat this seed?

if any, let him speak
for he shall I love[242]

who shall not love a tyrant dead
so well as liberty living?[243]

who is he, lean with hunger in the eyes
to take back his washed will and brain
from caesar's will that he may freely
think much his thrall to be too much?[244]

had you rather tyranny were living
and we all die slaves
than a caesar were dead
that we all live free men?[245]

if any, speak,
for him have I loved[246]

who is he who would fain freedom,
to have it,
loathe to lay his hands off it,
to refuse it,
the touch of it?[247]
who is he not of wood,
brick, mortar, the sickle,
the shelve, the spade, the ox
the fork, pitched that doth bear
us hard, inflamed and made mad?

who is he who knows 'tis good
he is not heir to these things
but men, bidders not the will
of caesar's will?[248]

who is he that loves freedom
more than he fears slavery?[249]

if any, speak,
for he shall I love[250]

romans, countrymen, black men,[251]
hath thou rather a tyrant live
and we all die slaves than
a caesar meets his death
that we all live free men?[252]

if there be any,
let him speak,
for he shall I love[253]

STRONG

it's just a matter of
living and dying,
life and death,

we are not strong,
the strong face death
but once[254]

courageous? we are too weak
and cowardly to die

we slither, slide in places more void
and there hide to let courage pass us by[255]

we settle for living our lives
cowards to die cowardly
many times before our deaths[256]

we are not strong

SUFFERANCE

founding fathers' iniquities
perditious spirits[257] aswirl
no virtue interred in their bones,[258]
the evils they did live after them

their yoke, our sufferance,
show us to be slaves still,
show us to be shuffling faces on
screams falling on death's ears
we've not walked a free man's day
without the wears of their oppression[259]

we've been governed not by what they've
declared but what they've failed to openly
declare but did and do so in actions openly

vicars of human heist, human traffickers,
begetters of pillage and plunder,
christ-like poltergeist ghostwriters
ghostwriting constitutional apparitions
of fictitious emancipation

we're not governed by democracy but
phantom representation by representatives
misrepresenting, preempting a preamble'd
Constitution[260]lacking constitution

founding fathers' iniquities, sired seeds
sown in the marrow of their sons,
no virtues interred in their bones,[261]
their fathers, who aren't in heaven,[262] aren't dead
we're governed by their yokes,
the sufferance of our souls[263] shows us to be slaves still
we've not walked a free man's day
without the wears of their oppression[264]

TEMPERS AND TEMPERAMENT

outrageous, outlandish, over-the-top
founding fathers' tempers[265] want
black fathers of black cash-cow youths
to have that jackie robinson temperance[266]
incorporated to their founding attempts[267]

not that temper and temperament[268] of the
tenacious trembles of the tiber's tempest[269]
laVar ball,[270] proudly touting a father's baller
sons for their rightful monetary sum

not that genius temper and temperament
of richard williams,[271] that black father innovator
the white pay-to-learn-to-play tennis cartel
feared[272] lost revenues in williams revealing
parental pathways to develop tennis talent

what composition, disposition of black
predisposes a black man to be branded
a good jackie robinson black father defined
by the ill-tempers of white slave holders

outrageous, outlandish, over the top,
a marked slave, I need not hold up my left hand
as such for they've colored me well by sight[273]

white tempers defining, opining the composition,
disposition of black to mark as an outrageous, outlandish,
over-the-top negro, sentenced, shackled the imposition
of media character assassination by white news outlets
parading misguided, misinformed, media-prepped,
made-for-white TV black mothers, grandmothers
depicted hard working, abandon, tearfully pleading
their black cash cow, have not calves to
to step back to go back to get that subpar,
sub-marginal, unemployable university degree
rather than get that return on investing years of black
athletic prowess, toiling, sweating in ill-tempered
plantation cotton fields of dreams without paydays,
making millions of dollars for universities in
TV generated revenues, alumni gifts and givings

outrageous, outlandish, over-the-top
founding fathers' tempers want
black fathers of black cash cow have nots
to have that jackie robinson temperance,

that black gift that keeps on giving

THE REALITY OF BLACK SPATIAL RELATIVITY

my bones have but labored to attain
to this hour[274] this little measure,[275]
a common slave[276]

dragged some depraved distant point behind
the starting line, then allowed to shuffle
forward to some ill-defined consigned point,
still far behind the starting line where
the sign on the fence that fences us in
still reads plantation

we've been had, hoodwinked,[277]
hijacked, ship-jacked still, blacken masses,
made to miss see movement as progress

we've been slipped the poisonous pill
of a visual treadmill distilled in a closing
of the first eye,[278] a turning of the second eye[279]
a blind black eye leading a blind black eye

sightless, we've been had, hoodwinked,[280]
hijacked, ship-jacked still, within the illusion
of inclusion mirage'd within exclusion

hoodwinked,[281] within the illusion of progress,
an apparition of progression poorly viewed
within the spin of relative forward motion of
relative points whose relativity clearly
reveals the hard line of slavery still
far behind the starting line of
consigned freedom and democracy

relative points of black reality hung
within spatial relativity of slavery still
distilled in a closing of the first eye,[282]
a turning of the second[283]

blind eyes leading blind eyes
that a slave not know the end
of his days' oppression[284]

THE STORM

unto the climates they point upon[285]
oceans swell and rage and[286] are[287] foamed[288] [289] to be,
I have seen[290] why[291] is[292] th' ambitious exalted,[293]

unto the perilous night[294]
this[295] storm is up and[296] not[297] I [298] to walk[299]
thus I, un-braced,[300] believe I[301] now[302]
this disturbed sky.[303]

I have seen[304] in[305] the why,[306]
tempests[307] blow wind, swell billow, and swim bark[308]
they[309] have bared my bosom
even to the thunderstone[310]

when the scolding winds
have rived the knotty oaks,
are you not moved?[311]

when the cross blue lightning opens
in the aim and the very flash of it,[312]
are you not moved?[313]

when all the way the sway of earth[314]
seems to[315] shake like a thing un-firm,[316]
why[317] are you not moved?[318]

THE STORM is composed using only words or phrases from the five excerpts from the play *Julius Caesar* referencing a storm. No new words were added to create the poem, none were eliminated. Each footnote indicates where each excerpted word or phrase originated.

The Five Excerpts:

1) I believe they are portentous things unto the climates that they point upon: Act 1, Scene 3, lines 31-32

2) Are you not moved when all the way the sway of earth shakes like a thing unfirm? I have seen tempests when the scolding winds have rived the knotty oaks, and I have seen th' ambitious ocean swell and rage and foam to be exalted with the threatening clouds:– Act1, Scene 3, lines 3-8

3) This disturbed sky is not to walk in: Act 1, Scene 3, lines 39-40

4) I unto the perilous night and thus un-braced, have bared my bosom to the thunder-stone. And when the cross blue lightning seemed to open even in the aim and very flash of it: Act 1, Scene 3, lines 48-53

5) Why, now, blow wind, swell billow, and swim bark! The storm is up and all is on the hazard: Act 5, Scene 1, lines 67-68

that Caesar,
this caesar

a beast without a heart,[319] *that* Caesar,
tyranny severs the head and hacks
the limbs in wrath and envy[320]

a heart within the beast,[321] its
fraternal twin democracy, *this* caesar
pushed from the same mother
at the same time of the same day,
basks in being the sacrificer,
not the butcher[322]

let me have no men about me that
cannot see the fraternity of these twins[323]

in both, life does waste life,[324]
both feast well upon our flesh[325]
and for this and this cause alone,
I rather tyranny be dead and we live
freemen than let democracy live
and we die slaves,[326] *this* caesar
is more dangerous than *that* Caesar[327]

for I know when thou didst hate *that* Caesar worst,
thou lovedst *this* caesar better than ever thou
lovedst the freedom it promised[328] and *this* love
is more dangerous than *that* hate

I shall never hate *that* Caesar living
as much as I love *this* caesar dead[329]

it is not that I love *that* Caesar living more,
but that I love more *this* caesar dead[330]

THREE CARD MONTY

this black man, this african,
this son of the motherland,
an undesirable refugee of european
colonies of ravenous rape and greed

this black man, this african,
this son of the motherland

hooded, housed a myriad of far east knickknacks
borne his backpack packed to capacity while afoot,
flat-footed in open sandals wandering european
dead end streets of closed offed opportunities

relegated, a shuffling con man street hustling
cheap chinese shit to white passersby,
what he doeth, the oppressor presses him to do[331]

relegated, a street hustling con man constrained to
con history's greatest con man in his monotone lands
of falsehoods and good white neighborhoods,
what he doeth, the oppressor presses him to do[332]

this black man, this African,
this son of the motherland,
this white man will never see you
a pilgrim of pilgrimage he claimed he was

when he discovered your land nor you a
christopher columbus, a ferdinand magellan [333]
when you would discover his white neighborhoods

you're a black man, an african, viewed
skewed a black contraband,[334] understood to
be an illegal african sighting, hooded in the
neighborhoods of the white man's lands
a three card monty shuffling,
playing up to how low the white man
on high looks down on you
shuffling, frantically street hustling
cheap chinese shit to white passersby

'TIS NEITHER HERE NOR THERE[335]

can't face who I am, I won't
wear the heart upon the sleeve
for daws to peck at [336]so I and all
to see the who of what I am

served a writ of right, I
can't face who I am changing face
to play Othello in black face, Jesus in white
'tis neither here nor there,[337]
can't face who I am, I am what I am

I can't face what I've become
won't undo, can't undo
what I have done
Judas I am,
shrouded in the shroud of Turin,[338]
weaved and woven by my own hands
to suit my motives

I am two faces, four tongues,
I play Othello in black face, Jesus in white
'tis neither here nor there[339]
I am what I am
I am what I have done

TILTING

executive, judicial, legislative,
three separate but equal branches of power
to keep the tilt towards liberty

but tilting towards liberty is not liberty

the three branches of power,
neither separate nor separated
they are a family web woven by
a genius spider of a common specie

the three branches are not separate nor separated
they are porous membranes bleeding profusely
across one another along similar streams of executive,
judicial, and legislative tribal blood types and lines

they nominate one another
based on blood types
they vote for one another
based on tribal lines
they make laws to benefits one another
based on blood types
they sit in prejudicial judgment of one another
based on tribal lines
empower one another to enrich one another
along blood lines

they, the gang of three, are condemned
to have an itching palm to sell and mart
their offices for gold to under-servers[340]

they contaminate their fingers with base bribes
and sell the mighty space of their large honors
for so much trash as may be grasped thus[341]

the three separate branches of power are not separate,
each blood line conspires with the other
based on mutual tribal, political beliefs
to establish and coalesce power

three separate branches,
executive, judicial, and legislative,
cunningly, constantly titling us towards liberty,
knowing tilting towards liberty is not liberty

WHAT POLITICS HAS A SLAVE?

what politics has a slave?

let us not sleep with the knights of white
and have about us sly-headed men,
lean and hungry, whose thoughts slither
more than they think, who hide their
true face in their darkness[342]

speak us our beliefs; that bloody afterbirth
of long lived and labored post-term freedom
prolonged beneath his politics for we to say
it is our politics

such thoughts slither more than they think,
for what politics has a slave?

such slithering is to make us believe
solutions to our problems lie within
the knights of white's subverted
political parties, politics, and politicians

such thoughts slither more than
they think and are but tools to
befool, to make fools of us, to keep trained
our minds that politics have enslaved

for what politics has a slave
plundered four hundred years?
what politics speaks a slave
when rome all aglow burns below
our feet and between our toes?[343]

when black politics fall oblivious the cochleae
of white knights around the jim crow white table

when black politics fail to repatriate that
one-way highway back down liberation

what politics has a slave?

WHITE MAN'S INTELLECT

cassius's intellect was not caesar's wisdom,
thus caesar his fall,
his statue and stature to weep like a
fountain with a thousand spouts[344] seeping
his blood as fast as it streamed forth[345]

no outcome pleased cassius so no means
of death caesar more pleasant then as
by cassius's intellect, reeked purpled;[346]
an apothecary's poison believed wisdom
caesar made to drink, thus his fall

white intellect is not a black man's
wisdom, thus his fallings

his dignity and stature weeping like a
fountain with a thousand spouts[347] seeping
his blood as fast as it streams forth[348]

no outcome pleases white so no means
of death black more pleasant then as
by white intellect, reeked and purpled;
an apothecary's poison believed wisdom the
black man is made to drink[349] thus his falling,
his four hundred year fall

WHITE

what should be in that name?

why should white be sounded
more than black?

sound them, both become
the mouth as well[350]

are we not two lions
littered in one day?[351]

why should white be sounded
more than black?

write them, together
black is as fair a name
written as white

is not morning, is not night
the same day?

same, man-made un-likes
are equals just the same[352]

stand them side by side
neither be higher, lower,
neither a shadow casts the other

weigh them, black is as heavy,
gravity pulls equally their name to ear

what then be in that name white
that it be sounded more than black?

YET I KNOW NOT

heard I,
amongst many of your best speaking of this, above all,
for the best for you,
their warnings having wished you had their eyes[353]

it's said I know not because
I have not a child, a parent I'm not

yet I have not said as much as your loving mother
of eleven who has said it more and plainer than I
and does either, not make her a parent

I have not said as much as your loving sister
who has said it more and plainer than I
and has she not one child and does that one
not make her a parent

yet I know not though my words
say the same as

is not my love of you more than
yet rendered less than because
it's said I have not a child and
as such I am not a parent

am I to be a husband to know
how to be as much as your man

we see things as they are
when we are ready to see

we hear things as they are
when we are ready to hear

short thereof, we see and hear
only what we want and need
to see, hear, to deny reality

I see as things are, needing not
to be rendered a parent nor anything
other than me as a basis for seeing

FOOTNOTES

1   Analysis of Political Morality in Shakespeare's 'Julius Caesar'
    https://medium.com/@kelsilynelle/analysis-of-political-morality-
    in-shakespeares-julius-caesar-18f57c0d4b4a
2   Act 1, Scene 2, lines 97 - 117
3   Ibid
4   Book of Common Prayer (1928), p. 337 [The Church Pension
    Fund]
5   Act 1, Scene 2, lines 97 - 117
6   Act 1, Scene 2, lines 119 - 120
7   Act 1, Scene 2, lines 97 - 117
8   Where members of the Roman Senate murdered Gaius Julius
    Caesar
9   Act 1, Scene 2, lines 192-195
10 Act 1, Scene 1, lines 33-34
11 Act 1, Scene 2, lines 192-195
12 Act 1, Scene 2, lines 192-195
13 Act 3, Scene 1, lines 163-166
14 Act 1, Scene 3, line 64
15 Act 3, Scene 1, lines 163-166
16 Act 3, Scene 2, lines 131-132
17 Act 3, Scene 1, lines 163-169
18 Act 4, Scene 3, lines 190-191
19 The boundary of the region of a black hole from which no escape
    is possible. https://en.wikipedia.org/wiki/Black_hole
20 Act 2, Scene 1, lines 2-3
21 Act 5, Scene 5, lines 41-42
22 Act 1, Scene 3, lines 83-85
23 Act 1, Scene 2, lines 35-37
24 Act 1, Scene 2, lines 97-98
25 Act 1, Scene 3, lines 83-85
26 Act 1, Scene 2, lines 208-209
27 Act 3, Scene 2, lines 211-212
28 Act 1, Scene 2, lines 35-37
29 Act 1, Scene 2, line 16
30 Act 1, Scene 3, lines 83-85

[31] Act 3, Scene 2, lines 20-21
[32] Constitution of United States of America 1789 (rev. 1992)
[33] Act 3, Scene 1, lines 97-98
[34] Act 2, Scene 1, line 316
[35] Act 2, Scene 3, lines 5-6
[36] Act 1, Scene 3, lines 39-40
[37] Act 2, Scene 1, lines 14-15
[38] President Barack Obama
[39] Act 2, Scene 1, line 316
[40] Harry Truman
[41] Harry Truman
[42] Act 1, Scene 3, lines 39-40
[43] Constitution of United States of America 1789 (rev. 1992)
[44] Act 3, Scene 1, line 159
[45] Act 3, Scene 2, lines 20-21
[46] Act 3, Scene 2, line 72
[47] Act 3, Scene 1, lines 1-2
[48] Act 3, Scene 1, line 253
[49] Act 2, Scene 1, line 52
[50] Act 1, Scene 3, lines 39-40
[51] Act 2, Scene 1, lines 18-27
[52] Act 2, Scene 1, lines 18-27
[53] Act 2, Scene 1, lines 77-82
[54] Act 2, Scene 1, lines 228-230
[55] Ibid.
[56] Act 2, Scene 1, lines 18-27
[57] Act 3, Scene 1, lines 1-2
[58] Act 3, Scene 2, line 72
[59] Act 1, Scene 3, lines 102-104
[60] Act 1, Scene 3, lines 102-104
[61] Equitas or Aequitas, divinity of fairness. Roman of equality.
http://www.talesbeyondbelief.com/roman-gods/roman-gods-list.htm
[62] Act 1, Scene 2, lines 227 and 235. Caesar was offered the crown
three times and each time, more reluctantly, declined it.
[63] Act 1, Scene 2, line 221
[64] Act 3, Scene 1, lines 157-166
[65] Act 3, Scene 2, lines 268-269
[66] Act 4, Scene 3, line 102
[67] Act 1, Scene 3, lines 108-109

[68] 1919 Supreme Court Ruling Schenck v. U.S. - Crying Fire in a Crowded Theater

[69] Act 1, Scene 2, lines 124-126

[70] 1969 United States Supreme Court, Brandenburg v. Ohio - Limiting 1st Amendment Rights

[71] This poem references not Julius Caesar, but Macbeth.

[72] Macbeth, Act 5, Scene 5, lines 19-29

[73] Ibid.

[74] Ibid.

[75] Ibid.

[76] Act 2, Scene 1, lines 14-15

[77] Note of hand- promissory note; a promise written and dated to pay a specified amount on demand or at a certain time. http://www.thefreedictionary.com/note+of+hand; https://www.collinsdictionary.com/us/dictionary/english/promissory-note

[78] Act 2, Scene 4, lines 44-45

[79] Act 2, Scene 3, line 133

[80] Act 3, Scene 1, line 288

[81] Slang meaning to treat with disrespect or contempt. (insult,https://www.merriam- webster.com/dictionary/diss).

[82] Alexander the Great's horse, www.pothos.org/content/indexaf1c.html?page=bucephalus

[83] A winged stallion in Greek methodology, www.greekmythology.com/Myths/Creatures/Pegasus/pegasus.html

[84] Act 3, Scene 2, lines 13-14

[85] The name of the Roman sword used in battle, www.darkknightarmoury.com/c-1419-roman-swords.aspx

[86] The Roman sword handle (hilt) has three parts: pommel, grip, and cross guard, www.reliks.com/functional-swords/types/gladius/; http://weaponsofchoice.com/extras/sword-parts-explained/

[87] Ibid.

[88] Ibid.

[89] Act 4, Scene 3, lines 167 168

[90] Alexander the Great's horse, www.pothos.org/content/indexaf1c.html?page=bucephalus

[91] A general in the army of Alexander the Great. He was Alexander's dearest friend throughout their lives. www.ancient.eu/Hephaestion/

[92] Patroclus was best friend to Achilles in Greek mythology,
www.greekmythology.com/Myths/Mortals/Patroclus/patroclus.html
[93] Italian for cutting,
www.freetranslation.com/en/translate-english-italian
[94] Italian for two cuttings,
www.freetranslation.com/en/translate-english-italian
[95] The name of the Roman sword used in battle,
www.darkknightarmoury.com/c-1419-roman-swords.aspx
[96] Act 1, Scene 3, lines 105-107
[97] Act 1, Scene 2, lines 136-147
[98] Act 1, Scene 3, lines 105-107
[99] Act 2, Scene 2, line 84
[100] Act 1, Scene 2, lines 54-55
[101] Act 5, Scene 5, lines 41-42
[102] Act 1, Scene 2, lines 35-37
[103] Act 1, Scene 2, lines 124-126
[104] Act 5, Scene 1, lines 84-88
[105] Act 1, Scene 2, lines 48-49
[106] Act 3, Scene 2, lines 13-14
[107] Act 2, Scene 1, line 59
[108] Act 1, Scene 2, lines 202-203
[109] Act 2, Scene 1, lines 145-150
[110] Act 2, Scene 2, lines 76-80
[111] Act 3, Scene 1, lines 157-166
[112] Act 2, Scene 2, line 84
[113] Act 1, Scene 2, lines 54-55
[114] Act 1, Scene 3, lines 90-91
[115] Seen in a mirage; having the nature or appearance of a mirage,
https://en.oxforddictionaries.com/definition/miraged
[116] To mislead the mind or judgment of;
https://www.merriam-webster.com/dictionary/delusion
[117] An inability to distinguish between what is real and what only
seems to be real
https://www.merriam-webster.com/dictionary/delusion
[118] Martin Luther King's April 3, 1968 speech made the night before
his murder.
[119] 1776 U.S. Declaration of Independence
[120] 13th Amendment, US Constitution
[121] 4th Amendment, US Constitution
[122] 6th Amendment, US Constitution

[123] 1776 U.S. Declaration of Independence

[124] Ibid.

[125] Martin Luther King's April 3, 1968 speech made the night before his murder

[126] Martin Luther King's April 3' 1968 speech.

[127] Act 1, Scene 2, lines 192-195

[128] Act 2, Scene 1, line 245

[129] Martin Luther King's April 3' 1968 speech.

[130] Money and resources. color-coded access to social-economic advantages and benefits.

[131] Black Americans as a wealth building source of cheap labor and exploitation

[132] The institutions of entrenched white racist america

[133] Individuals comprising and running the institutions of entrenched white racist america

[134] Act 1, Scene 1, lines 37-41

[135] A trumpet made of a ram's horn, blown by the Hebrews as a signal for battle and religious ceremonies

[136] Act 1, Scene 1, lines 44-46

[137] Exposing the institutions and racist acts and intents

[138] Act 4, Scene 3, line 115

[139] Act 3, Scene 2, lines 140-144

[140] African American football quarterback shut out of the NFL for the crime of using his platform (taking a knee during the playing of the national anthem) to protest the killing of black kids by police.
https://www.thenation.com/article/nfls-war-colin-kaepernick/

[141] Act 1, Scene 1, line 52

[142] Adaptation of 'Faith without works is dead.'
https://www.compellingtruth.org/faith-without-works-dead.html

[143] Act 1, Scene 1, line 8

[144] Act 3, Scene 2, lines 13-14

[145] Act 3, Scene 2, lines 185-186

[146] Act 4, Scene 3, lines 27-28

[147] Act 1, Scene 1, lines 44-46

[148] Act 3, Scene 2, lines 13-14

[149] Act 1, Scene 3, lines 90-101

[150] JFK's Presidential Inaugural Address, January 20, 1961

[151] Ibid.

[152] Act 4, Scene 3, lines 27-28

[153] The Roman sword
[154] 1776 U.S. Declaration of Independence
[155] JFK's Presidential Inaugural Address, 1.20.61
[156] Act 1, Scene 3, lines 90-101
[157] A vagrant samurai without a master,
https://www.merriam-webster.com/dictionary/ronin
[158] Act 1, Scene 2, lines 60-64
[159] Post on the liberal lawns of the appalling silent
[160] What is Frankincense,
https://www.thoughtco.com/what-is-frankincense-700747
[161] Act 1, Scene 2, lines 60-64
[162] Ibid
[163] Act 1, Scene 2, lines 136–147
[164] Ibid
[165] Ibid.
[166] Act 1, Scene 2, lines 136-147. Men at some time are masters of
their fates. The fault, dear Brutus, is not in our stars but in
ourselves that we are underlings–
[167] Ibid.
[168] Act 2, Scene 2, lines 46-48
[169] Act 3, Scene 2, line 177
[170] Polish for "at once".
[171] Act 2, Scene 2, lines 1-2
[172] Act 2, Scene 2, line 116
[173] Act 1, Scene 3, lines 156-158
[174] Act 1, Scene 2, lines 17-19
[175] Act 1, Scene 2, lines 89-91
[176] Act 2, Scene 2, line 116
[177] Act 2, Scene 1, lines 145-150
[178] Act 1, Scene 1, lines 71-73
[179] Act 2, Scene 2, line 116
[180] Act 1, Scene 2, line 2
[181] Act 1, Scene 3, lines 83-85
[182] Act 5, Scene 5, lines 41-42
[183] Polish for "at once"
[184] Act 1, Scene 1, lines 37-41
[185] Act 3, Scene 1, lines 157-166
[186] Act 1, Scene 2, lines 208-209
[187] Act 3, Scene 2, lines 247-248
[188] Act 1, Scene 2, lines 302-307

[189] Act 1, Scene 3, lines 145-148

[190] Act 1, Scene 2, lines 302-307

[191] Act 1, Scene 2, lines 60-64

[192] Act 1, Scene 2, lines 89-91

[193] Act 1, Scene 2, lines 60-64

[194] Act 1, Scene 2, lines 69-72

[195] Act 4, Scene 1, line 28

[196] Area of the horse's anatomy that defines its "back" and where the saddle sits. https://sites.psu.edu/alexaugust19/2015/11/06/external-equine-anatomy/

[197] Act 2, Scene 1, line 254

[198] Act 4, Scene 1, line 28

[199] Act 5, Scene 1, lines 122-125

[200] Act 1, Scene 2, lines 17-19

[201] Act 1, Scene 2, lines 124-126

[202] Act 2, Scene 1, line 113

[203] Act 3, Scene 1, lines 115-117

[204] Act 1, Scene 2, lines 17-19

[205] Act 3, Scene 1, lines 80-83

[206] The name of Paul Revere's horse, https://generalaviationnews.com/2007/03/23/do-you-know-the-name-of-paul-reveres-horse/

[207] Act 3, Scene 1, Lines 137-138

[208] 1776 U.S. Declaration of Independence

[209] Malcolm X's 1964 Speech at the Founding Rally of the Organization of Afro-American Unity, http://www.blackpast.org/1964-malcolm-x-s-speech-founding-rally-organization-afro-american-unity#sthash.AbFPa18Y.dpuf

[210] A mountain in Tennessee referred to by MLK in his "I Have A Dream" speech

[211] Act 1, Scene 2, line 21

[212] Act 1, Scene 2, line 54

[213] Act 3, Scene 2, lines 247-248

[214] Act 1, Scene 2, lines 92-93

[215] Act 3, Scene 1, lines 31-32

[216] Act 2, Scene 2, line18

[217] Act 1, Scene 2, lines 89-91

[218] Transitive verb: To place (as oneself) under an obligation (as of returning something borrowed)
https://www.merriam-webster.com/dictionary/indebt

[219] A latin adage translated "If you want peace, prepare for war." It has been adapted from Book 3 of the Latin author Publius Flavius Vegetius Renatus's De Re Militari (4th or 5th century) "si wis pake para bellu"

[220] Act 1, Scene 2, lines 17-19

[221] Act 3, Scene 2, lines 20-21

[222] Act 2, Scene 1, lines 46-47

[223] Act 2, Scene 1, line 113

[224] Act 2, Scene 1, line 107

[225] Act 3, Scene 2, lines 176-177

[226] Act 2, Scene 1, lines 183-185

[227] Act 1, Scene 2, lines 211-212

[228] Act 1, Scene 2, lines 17-19

[229] A latin adage translated – "If you want peace, prepare for war." It has been adapted from Book 3 of the Latin author Publius Flavius Vegetius Renatus's De Re Militari (4th or 5th century)

[230] Jesus of Lübeck–Slave Shiphttps://en.wikipedia.org/wiki/Slave_ship

[231] Ibid Madre de Deus (Mother of God), slave ship

[232] Ibid Henrietta Marie.slave ship

[233] Ibid Duc Du Maine, slave ship (1719)

[234] Act 3, Scene 1, lines 115-117

[235] In the 1975 Paramount film Mandingo, a "Mandingo" represents the finest stock of slaves deemed most suitable for fighting and breeding. https://muse.jhu.edu/article/170732/pdf and https://en.wikipedia.org/wiki/Mandingo_(film)

[236] Men who plotted to kill Julius Caesars, Act 3, Scene 1, lines 1-2

[237] Act 3, Scene 2, lines 26-32

[238] Act 3, Scene 1, lines 1-2

[239] Act 3, Scene 2, lines 13-14

[240] Act 1, Scene 2, line 8

[241] Act 1, Scene 2, lines 89-91

[242] Act 3, Scene 2, lines 26-32

[243] Act 3, Scene 1, lines 137-138

[244] Act 1, Scene 2, lines 192-195

[245] Act 3, Scene 2, lines 22-23

[246] Act 3, Scene 2, lines 26-32

[247] Act 1, Scene 2, lines 234-244
[248] Act 3, Scene 2, lines 26-32
[249] Act 1, Scene 2, lines 89-91
[250] Act 3, Scene 2, lines 26-32
[251] Act 3, Scene 2, lines 13-14
[252] Act 3, Scene 2, lines 22-23
[253] Act 3, Scene 2, lines 26-32
[254] Act 2, Scene 2, lines 32-33
[255] Act 2, Scene 4, lines 5-6
[256] Act 2, Scene 2, lines 32-33
[257] Act 1, Scene 3, lines 83-85
[258] Act 3, Scene 2, line 74
[259] Act 1, Scene 1, lines 3-5
[260] Basic written set of principles and precedents of federal government in the US. Ratified in 1789, the Constitution has since been modified by twenty-six amendments. https://en.oxforddictionaries.com/definition/constitution
[261] Act 3, Scene 2, line 74
[262] Luke 11:2-4
[263] Act 2, Scene 1, lines 115-117
[264] Act 1, Scene 1, lines 3-5
[265] Habit of mind, especially with respect to irritability orpatience, outbursts of anger, or the like disposition; https://www.dictionary.com/browse/temper?s=t
[266] Moderation or self-restraint in action, statement, etc.; self-control; https://www.dictionary.com/browse/temperance
[267] Act 1 Scene 3, lines 136-137
[268] The act or process of tempering or modifying; https://www.merriam-webster.com/dictionary/temperament
[269] Act 1, Scene 1, line 46
[270] Proud father of Basketball Player Alonzo Ball
[271] Father of tennis greats Venus and Serena Williams
[272] https://www.theshadowleague.com/story/lavar-ball-and-the-role-of-the-black-sports-father
[273] Act 1, Scene 3, lines 295-297
[274] Act 5, Scene 5, lines 41-42
[275] Act 3, Scene 1, line 154
[276] Act 1, Scene 3, lines 15-18

277 Excerpt Malcolm X Speech, https://denzealotdata.wordpress.com/2016/06/19/malcolm-x-speech-excerpt/

278 Sensory input such as sight: https://en.wikipedia.org/wiki/Third_eye

279 The eye of reason, meditation, and reflection: https://en.wikipedia.org/wiki/Third_eye

280 Malcolm X Speech, https://denzealotdata.wordpress.com/2016/06/19/malcolm-x-speech-excerpt/

281 Malcolm X Speech, https://denzealotdata.wordpress.com/2016/06/19/malcolm-x-speech-excerpt/

282 Sensory input such as sight; https://en.wikipedia.org/wiki/Third_eye

283 The eye of reason, meditation, and reflection: https://en.wikipedia.org/wiki/Third_eye

284 Act 5, Scene 1, lines 124-127

285 Act 1, Scene 3, lines 31-32

286 Act 1, Scene 3, lines 3-8

287 Act 1, Scene 3, lines 31-32

288 Act 1, Scene 3, lines 3-8

289 Act 1, Scene 3, lines 31-32

290 Act 1, Scene 3, lines 3-8

291 Act 5, Scene 1, lines: 67-68

292 Act 1, Scene 3, lines 39-40

293 Act 1, Scene 3, lines 3-8

294 Act 1, Scene 3, lines 48-53

295 Act 1, Scene 3, lines 39-40

296 Act 5, Scene 1, lines 67-68

297 Act 1, Scene 3, lines 39-40

298 Act 1, Scene 3, lines 31-32

299 Act 1, Scene 3, lines 39-40

300 Act 1, Scene 3, lines 48-53

301 Act 1, Scene 3, lines 31-32

302 Act 5, Scene 1, lines 67-68

303 Act 1, Scene 3, lines 39-40

304 Act 1, Scene 3, lines 3-8

305 Act 1, Scene 3, lines 39-40

306 Act 5, Scene 1, lines 67-68

[307] Act 5, Scene 3, lines 3-8

[308] Act 5, Scene 1, lines 67-68

[309] Act 1, Scene 3, lines 31-32

[310] Act 1, Scene 3, lines 48-53

[311] Act 1, Scene 3, lines 3-8

[312] Act 1, Scene 3, lines 48-53

[313] Act 1, Scene 3, lines 3-8

[314] Act 1, Scene 3, lines 3-8

[315] Act 1, Scene 3, lines 48-53

[316] Act 1, Scene 3, lines 3-8

[317] Act 5, Scene 1, lines 67-68

[318] Act 1, Scene 3, lines 3-8

[319] Act 2, Scene 2, line 42

[320] Act 2, Scene 1, lines 165-166

[321] Act 2, Scene 2, line 40

[322] Act 2, Scene 1, line 168

[323] Act 1, Scene 2, lines 192-195

[324] Act 2, Scene 1, line 59

[325] Act 1, Scene 2, lines 100-101

[326] Act 3, Scene 2, lines 22-23

[327] Act 2, Scene 2, lines 45-48

[328] Act 4, Scene 3, lines 104-111

[329] Act 3, Scene 1, lines 137-138

[330] Act 3, Scene 2, lines 13-14

[331] Act 2, Scene 4, lines 44-45

[332] Ibid.

[333] Ferdinand Magellan led the first expedition to circumnavigate the globe and is thought to be the first European to cross the Pacific Ocean. http://exploration.marinersmuseum.org/subject/ferdinand-magellan/

[334] Definitions of contraband: 1.A slave who during the American Civil War escaped to or was brought within the Union lines. 2. goods or merchandise whose importation, exportation, or possession is forbidden. https://www.merriam-webster.com/dictionary/contraband

[335] *Othello*, Act 4, Scene 3, line 58, Emilia and Desdemona discuss marriage, husbands, and fidelity. Desdemona cries and asks if Emilia minds her crying. Emilia responds: 'Tis neither here nor there, meaning that it doesn't matter to

her.http://www.cliffsnotes.com/literature/o/othello/study-help/top-5-quotes-explained

[336] *Othello*, Act 1, Scene 1, lines 64-65). Protagonist Iago reveals he will manipulate and act deceptively if it suits his motives. http://www.cliffsnotes.com/literature/o/othello/study-help/top-5-quotes-explained; http://www.enotes.com/homework-help/what-does-iago-mean-when-he-say-but-will-weqar-my-282292

[337] *Othello*, Act 4, Scene 3, line 58

[338] The cloth bearing the image of that believed to be the burial shroud of Jesus of Nazareth. https://en.wikipedia.org/wiki/Shroud_of_Turin

[339] Othello, Act 4, Scene 3, line 58

[340] Act 4, Scene 2, lines 22-24

[341] Act 4, Scene 3, lines 24-26

[342] Act 2, Scene 1, lines 280-289

[343] Act 2, Scene 1, lines 46-47

[344] Act 2, Scene 2, lines 76-80

[345] Act 3, Scene 1, lines 204-205

[346] Act 3, Scene 1, lines 157-166

[347] Act 2, Scene 2, lines 76-80

[348] Act 3, Scene 1, lines 204-205

[349] Act 3, Scene 1, lines 157-166

[350] Act 1, Scene 2, lines 136-147

[351] Act 2, Scene 2, lines 45-48

[352] Act 2, Scene 2, line 129

[353] Act 1, Scene 2, lines 60-64

CPSIA information can be obtained
at www.ICGtesting.com
Printed in the USA
LVHW111600230320
650924LV00005B/40/J

9 789176 375884